Be Happy

A Little Book of Mindfulness

To my wonderful family
and Hucky x
MB

For Justin—you are my hero.
With love x
ED

Be Happy
A Little Book of Mindfulness

Maddy Bard

illustrated by
Emma Dodd

Be Happy

Hucky and Buzz love to run in the park
and feel the grass under their paws.
What do you like to do?

Be Thankful

Hucky and Buzz appreciate the little things.

Look at the beautiful world around you.

What are you thankful for?

Be Kind

Kindness makes everyone feel better
and can be shown in lots of different ways.
What kind things can you do?

Show Love

Being loved is a happy feeling.

It makes us feel warm inside.

Give someone a big hug to show them you care!

Breathe

Sometimes Hucky and Buzz sit quietly
and listen to the sound of their breathing.

Put your hand on your tummy and breathe in slowly through your nose, then out through your mouth. How does it make you feel?

Believe in Yourself
With self-confidence,
you can do amazing things!

Feel Your Feelings

Sometimes it's OK to not feel OK.

Talk to Someone

When Hucky and Buzz are worried or sad,
they talk to each other.

Stay Positive

You never know what will happen tomorrow—

maybe something great!

Hucky and Buzz enjoy the surprises each day brings.

Keep Busy

Hucky and Buzz are happiest when they
have plans for the day.

What are some of the ways you keep busy?

Be Patient

Hucky and Buzz know that good things come if they wait.

Try Something Different

Learning new tricks is fun.
What new things will you try?

Slow Down

Hucky and Buzz love racing around, but they know that taking time to relax is important too.

Play!

Hucky and Buzz are always laughing and playing.
Smiling can make you feel happier, so . . .

have fun!

First US edition 2023
First published by Templar Books, an imprint of Bonnier Books UK, 2023

Library of Congress Catalog Card Number 2022908692
ISBN 978-1-5362-2976-9

22 23 24 25 26 27 LEO 10 9 8 7 6 5 4 3 2

Printed in Heshan, Guangdong, China

This book was typeset in Mrs Lollipop and Brandon Grotesque.
The illustrations were created digitally.

TEMPLAR BOOKS
an imprint of
Candlewick Press
99 Dover Street
Somerville, Massachusetts 02144

www.candlewick.com